W9-BUO-008

OCT -- 2011

First Facts®

Best of Pro Sports

The Best of Figure Skating

by Kathy Allen

Consultant:
Karen Cover
Museum Archivist
World Figure Skating Museum & Hall of Fame
Colorado Springs, Colorado

CAPSTONE PRESS
a capstone imprint

First Facts is published by Capstone Press,
151 Good Counsel Drive, P.O. Box 669, Mankato, Minnesota 56002.
www.capstonepress.com

Printed in the United States of America in North Mankato, Minnesota
092009
005618CGS10

Books published by Capstone Press are manufactured with paper
containing at least 10 percent post-consumer waste.

Library of Congress Cataloging-in-Publication Data
Allen, Kathy.
   The best of figure skating / by Kathy Allen.
   p. cm. — (First facts, best of pro sports)
   Includes bibliographical references and index.
   Summary: "Presents some of the best moments and skaters in figure skating
history" — Provided by publisher.
   ISBN 978-1-4296-3333-8 (library binding)
   1. Figure skating — History — Juvenile literature. 2. Figure skaters — Biography —
Juvenile literature. I. Title. II. Series.
 GV850.4.A44 2010
 796.91'209 — dc22   2009001175

Editorial Credits

Mari Bolte and Christopher Harbo, editors; Kyle Grenz, designer; Eric Gohl,
   media researcher; Eric Manske, production specialist

Photo Credits

AP Images/Amy Sancetta, 19; Doug Mills, 20; Mark Baker, 17 (right); Misha Japaridze, 18
BigStockPhoto.com/Morozova Tatiana, 1
Comstock Images, ice skates
CORBIS/TempSport/Jean-Yves Ruszniewski, 8
Getty Images Inc./AFP, 5; AFP/Daniel Janin, 15 (right); AFP/Juha Jormanainen,
   15 (left); AFP/Yuri Kadobnov, cover; Allsport/Clive Brunskill, 13; Allsport/
   Shaun Botterill, 7 (right); Bob Thomas, 17 (left); Clive Brunskill, 7 (left); Clive
   Rose, 11 (all)
Shutterstock/GoodMood Photo, skating rink background; Pertusinas, tickets

Essential content terms are **bold** and are defined at the bottom of the spread where they first appear.

Table of Contents

Best Olympic Moment

In 1968, the world watched the first Olympics shown live on TV. All eyes were on Peggy Fleming. She floated across the ice. Her graceful programs made her the darling of figure skating. Fancy footwork helped Fleming win gold. It was the only gold medal won by the United States at the 1968 Winter Olympics.

Best Come-From-Behind Win

United States skater Sarah Hughes shocked the world at the 2002 Olympics. She was in fourth place going into the **long program**. No one thought she could win gold. Hughes landed every jump, including two triple jump combinations. Her gold medal was one of the biggest upsets in Olympic history.

Tara Lipinski was just 15 years old when she won Olympic gold for the United States. In her 1998 long program, she landed every jump. Lipinski passed teammate Michelle Kwan for the gold.

long program: the longer of two programs in competition that shows the skater's skill, grace, and jumping ability

Best Jump Not Allowed in Competition

The backflip is not allowed in competition. Why? Because it can't usually be landed on one foot. But don't tell that to Surya Bonaly. The French national champion could land her backflip on one foot. It's not a legal jump, but it's fun to watch!

Best Pair Move

In 2004, Tatiana Totmianina and Max Marinin suffered a terrible fall. While performing the lasso lift, Totmianina crashed to the ice. Less than two years later, they performed the same move at the Olympics. The crowd held its breath. Marinin twirled Totmianina above his head. She landed perfectly. Their program won them the gold medal.

Is it a Tie?

At the 2006 Olympics, Totmianina and Marinin also performed the death spiral. He spun her in circles around him. Was the death spiral better than the lasso lift?

Best Pair Performance

In the 1994 Olympics, Ekaterina Gordeeva and Sergei Grinkov's bond was clear. The married couple skated perfectly to "Moonlight Sonata."

The romance in their skating wowed the crowd. They won a second gold medal. But their joy soon turned to sadness. Grinkov died suddenly less than two years later.

Best Crowd-Pleaser

Figure skating crowds loved Scott Hamilton. He won every world and U.S. championship from 1981 to 1984. He also won gold at the 1984 Olympics. In **exhibition** shows, fans loved Hamilton's humor and backflip jump. After he retired, Hamilton continued entertaining audiences as both a TV announcer and skater.

exhibition: a public display where skaters show off their skills

In the 1980s, Katarina Witt was the most popular female figure skater. The beauty from East Germany won Olympic gold twice. Her flashy costumes and stunning moves dazzled crowds. Witt was always happy to meet with fans.

Best Ice Dancing Performance

Jayne Torvill and Christopher Dean's 1984 Olympic **free dance** was stunning. Skating to "Bolero," the British pair circled the ice to the haunting music. Dean spun Torvill through twists and turns. They landed on the ice in a graceful finish. With perfect artistic scores, Torvill and Dean took the gold medal.

American ice dancers had not won an Olympic medal for 30 years. In 2006, Tanith Belbin and Ben Agosto put an end to that streak. Their flashy program was not perfect. But they won the silver. The wait for an American medal was over.

free dance: a performance where skaters choose their own music, themes, and movements

Best Rivalry

Johnny Weir and Evan Lysacek's **rivalry** is between artist and athlete. The **artistic** Weir won the U.S. national championships in 2004, 2005, and 2006.

rivalry: a fierce feeling of competition between two people

artistic: having or showing talent or skill

The athletic Lysacek answered by winning in 2007. At the national championships in 2008, they both scored 244.77 points. Lysacek's long program earned him a higher score, breaking the tie.

Best Comeback

Fans were shocked when Nancy Kerrigan was attacked before the 1994 Olympics. They suspected the attacker had been sent by skater Tonya Harding. With an injured knee, Kerrigan still competed against Harding in the Olympics. Fans cheered when she won the silver. Harding finished eighth.

Glossary

artistic (ar-TIS-tic) — having or showing talent or skill

exhibition (ek-suh-BI-shuhn) — a public display where skaters show off their skills

free dance (FREE danss) — a performance where skaters choose their own music, themes, and movements

long program (LONG PROH-gram) — the longer of two programs in competition that shows the skater's skill, grace, and jumping ability

rivalry (RYE-val-ree) — a fierce feeling of competition between two people

Read More

Jones, Jen. *Figure Skating For Fun!* For Fun. Minneapolis: Compass Point Books, 2006.

Thomas, Keltie. *How Figure Skating Works.* How Sports Work. Berkeley, Calif.: Owlkids, 2009.

Preston, David Curtis. *A World-Class Ice Skater.* The Making of a Champion. Chicago: Heinemann, 2005.

Internet Sites

FactHound offers a safe, fun way to find Internet sites related to this book. All of the sites on FactHound have been researched by our staff.

Here's all you do:

Visit *www.facthound.com*

FactHound will fetch the best sites for you!